GET THE MESSAGE

GET THE MESSAGE

A BUSINESS GUIDE TO

Surviving
THE
Email Security Crisis

TOM GILLIS

MNP
MESSAGING
NEWS PRESS

SPECIAL THANKS
to Paul Gargaro,
Stephanie Jordan, and Beth Cole.

CONTENTS

Part I
EMAIL: CAN'T LIVE WITH IT. CAN'T LIVE WITHOUT IT.

Part II
EMAIL: RULES, REGULATIONS AND LIABILITIES.

Part III
EMAIL: A MISSION-CRITICAL FUTURE.

FORWARD
GET THE MESSAGE.

The Email Explosion: From Humble Beginnings to Killer App.

In a society grown blasé over incremental techno-logical breakthroughs, email has emerged as a profound advancement in the way we communi-cate. Indeed, email has had such an extraordinary impact that, like the Fax and ATM, it's hard to imagine life before its widespread adoption in recent years. Email's exponential expansion has even the most circumspect business managers convinced that its popularity is no mere novelty, but rather a communications resource of bound-less application and value.

And more than a few complications.

Widespread Adoption Leads to Challenges

With the propagation of email into hundreds of millions of homes and businesses around the globe, the question is no longer "Do you have email?" but rather "What's your address?" This dramatic shift, however, has raised a multitude of challenges, stemming from email's asynchronous, one-to-many capability, accessibility, immediacy and shelf life.

Email today is under siege, and as users clamor to harness its potential, they have only a fragile framework in place regulating its use, protecting their privacy, and safeguarding their networks. Waves of spam are inundating system servers and user mailboxes, rendering far too many email addresses virtually unusable, while raising fresh fears of fraud and eroding consumer confidence in e-commerce.

Corporate email networks, which have mushroomed in size and importance to rival existing voice networks, remain alarmingly susceptible to virus attacks and crippling outages, while an unformulated policy over email storage has resulted in a string of smoking guns in several high-profile corporate legal battles. As a result, a collection of state and federal legislative solutions are vying to address these challenges, and promote better applications of this invaluable communications tool.

Bold New Ideas

The email revolution comes on the heels of a long series of electronic communication advances over the last 150 years, each helping to shrink the world in remarkable ways, while introducing a wondrous new realm of productivity. With the creation of the telegraph in the mid-19th century, up to 50 words a minute in Samuel Morse's code could travel hundreds or even thousands of miles via telegraph line. Not long after a new era in human correspondence emerged as Alexander Graham Bell gave his historic summons, "Mr. Watson come here..." spoken over the first, crude telephone. In the decades that followed, engineers deployed successive waves of telephonic advances to increase communication capability, ranging from the multi-line hand-set to teleconferencing, the PBX to voicemail and eventually to the liberating portability of today's wireless cellular networks.

> **FAST FACT:**
> ## Email Volume
> The total number of email messages sent across the Internet every day is greater than 30 billion. Unfortunately, more than 70% is spam.

Email's Early Days

With roots dating back to the early 1970s, email didn't gain traction in the marketplace for another decade when corporations began using the Internet to connect departmental mail servers. By the 1990s, new web-based systems brought email to the masses. Email's widespread acceptance has since had an enormous impact on commerce, increasing the speed and efficiency of doing business and slashing expenses. Billions of dollars change hands daily via e-commerce; bids are submitted, won and lost over the Internet; and customers' service questions are answered without the sender or the recipient ever leaving their desks.

DEFINITION:

Simple Mail Transfer Protocol (SMTP) functions similarly to a standard mail envelope with destination and return addresses. SMTP servers deliver and receive email using SMTP language embedded in each message's header.

Open Pathways Mean Greater Vulnerability

Based on a Simple Mail Transfer Protocol, or SMTP, the current email infrastructure was developed in an era when the Internet was largely the realm of scientists and academics, exchanging

ideas through a web of unreliable network connections. At the time, the Internet was a simpler,
friendlier place—a domain where identity theft
and fraud seemed inconceivable. Under SMTP,
messages are sent in clear, unencrypted text from
one machine to the next, with any mail gateway
acting as a relay to accept and pass messages
along. As email use has grown, SMTP has revealed
glaring susceptibility to fraudulent, infected and
unsolicited emails, which routinely mask their
identities. The commercial potential for illicit
email use has encouraged the exploitation of
SMTP's open pathways, with devastating results
for individual users and corporate networks.

Email's Future

While well-intentioned legislation moves to shore
up these vulnerabilities, the best hope for the
future of email rests in systematic, innovative
changes to the current protocol to discern friend
from foe. These infrastructure enhancements will
protect recipients' interests by clearly establishing
a sender's identity and providing receiving email
servers with a reliable gauge of that sender's
reputation.

In the brief period since its far-reaching

deployment in the marketplace, email has displayed an unprecedented capacity for facilitating communication, as well as marketing goods and services. Current system flaws and uncertainties may hamper email's progress in the short-term, but the medium's proven value ensures that intelligent solutions will emerge to protect and promote its long-term role in society.

How to Use This Book

Get the Message attempts to frame the complexities and issues surrounding email.

Email: Can't Live With It. Can't Live Without It. The first part of this book is dedicated to email basics and describing spam and computer viruses. The goal is to provide the reader with the status of email today and offer a foundation of understanding.

Email: Rules, Regulations and Liabilities. This section looks at the variety of regulations and policies that have emerged as email becomes more relied upon as a communication tool. Issues such as to what extent are corporations responsible for monitoring their employees' email use, and are businesses responsible for preventing offensive email from reaching their staff? We look at how new legislation affects the way marketers communicate with customers, and what steps business owners can take to secure their vital computer networks.

Email: A Mission-Critical Future. These chapters address the attributes of tomorrow's email infrastructure and how investment in email infrastructure can be shaped to help businesses keep up with the demand created by this rapidly evolving medium. We conclude the book with an important checklist of actions you can take to protect your network and your organization's reputation.

Part I

EMAIL:
CAN'T LIVE
WITH IT.
CAN'T LIVE
WITHOUT IT.

"Email is more
important to my
business
than voice
communication."

DOUG CARLYSLE
Managing Director, Menlo Ventures

1

EMAIL 101
UNDERSTANDING EMAIL BASICS.

E mail's rapid rise to ubiquity in the global marketplace has quickly converted users' curiosity about the medium's potential into a wholesale dependence on its capabilities. Based on the enormous volume of emails that stream through cyberspace daily, email correspondence has in practice become as routine as a phone call; simply type in the address, hammer out the message, and hit "send". Without question email today deserves its widespread moniker as the Internet's "Killer App."

A Brief History

The roots of email date back more than three decades when Ray Tomlinson—the acknowledged father of network email—sent the first message in 1971 via the ARPAnet network, an Internet precursor created by the Defense Department to link its research computing centers. It wasn't until the 1980s' proliferation of personal computers in the workplace and at home, however, that email's remarkable possibilities began to emerge. The subsequent development of a variety of email technologies — including bulletin boards and proprietary dial-up systems, which required both the sender and recipient to be subscribers — whetted the market's appetite for this new form of electronic interaction.

Local Area Networks

Businesses entered the email world by connecting their employees via Local Area Networks to facilitate internal company communication. By the close of the decade, the development of Eudora ushered in a groundbreaking, user-friendly interface for email management, and it was widely adopted in corporate and academic circles.

EMAIL TIMELINE

1971 - First email message sent

1980s - Personal PCs boost demand for expanded email technology

1990s - World Wide Web offers low-cost access and new opportunities

2000 - Email use skyrockets with popularity of web-based email systems

As the Medium Comes to the Masses

As the World Wide Web evolved in the 1990s, juggernauts like Microsoft and AOL began incorporating email technology into their browsers, helping to bring the medium to the masses with low-cost access and virtual interoperability.

Within the last half-decade, email use skyrocketed with the introduction of such web-based email systems as Hotmail, Yahoo! and others, which enable users to maintain free email accounts that can be accessed through a website by way of any networked computer.

How Email Works

Like computer technology itself, the mechanics of email are of less concern to today's typical user than the results they can produce. Yet with email's widespread adoption comes an array of issues that expose weaknesses in its current infrastructure and threaten its commercial acceptance. To fully appreciate the potential threats confronting email, it is essential to understand the basics of how messages are sent and received. From the casual user's perspective, how email circulates is a relatively simple concept. Create a message via your email client software or web-based service provider and send it off over the Internet. Yet there's much more to the process, and understanding how that process works can protect users from a variety of challenges that threaten legitimate email correspondence.

Email operates through what is known as the Simple Mail Transfer Protocol (SMTP), a two-way communications format that has been entrenched within the Internet's architecture since its introduction more than 30 years ago. SMTP functions in much the same way as a standard mail envelope, which features destination and return addresses. Using SMTP language embedded in each message's header, SMTP servers—through a simple series of commands and answers—are able to deliver and receive mail without having to examine the body of that message to determine its source or destination.

Email's Journey: From Sender to Recipient

It Begins. Email is composed on and launched from client software such as Lotus Notes, Microsoft Outlook, Outlook Express, Eudora, or Pegasus. It's typically addressed as follows: `recipient@theirdomain.com`. The mailer hits "Send" and communication is commenced.

First Stop. The email travels to the SMTP relay server for the sender's host account, which then contacts a Domain Name Server (DNS) to obtain the IP address for the recipient's domain name. In other words, the server actually has to locate the email server handling the recipient's email address, which is typed in as part of the recipient's address to the right of the @ symbol.

On Its Way. Once located, the Internet Protocol (IP) address is sent back to the sender's relay server, which, in turn, transfers the message to the email server at the recipient's domain address. This server then delivers the message to the recipient's account at a message store, otherwise known as a POP (Post Office Protocol) or IMAP (Internet Mail Access Protocol) server, which receives, routes and stores incoming mail. Corporations typically utilize Microsoft Exchange or IBM/Lotus Domino servers, which provide mail storage in conjunction with calendar and collaboration services.

Destination Reached. The recipient then accesses his or her email by launching their client software (Microsoft Outlook, Lotus Notes, Eudora, Outlook Express, etc.), which requests that the message store server deliver all email for their account to their computer to be read and archived at their leisure. Messages may be stored on the client machine, the message store, or both.

Email Addresses

The process for addressing email messages borrows from traditional mail standards where the destination `(To:)` and source `(From:)` of the message are indicated on the envelope. In email, this "envelope" information is first read by the SMTP relays, which route and deliver messages. An email's envelope address, however, is often different from the header address that appears in client mail readers such as Outlook. This alteration enables a host provider to forward the mail. For example, the email envelope's source information may read: `generalmotors@gm.net`, but the message shows up in the client viewer as being from `customerservice@generalmotors.com`.

Why SMTP Was Revolutionary, and Why We Have Outgrown It

The Internet was in an embryonic stage when Ray Tomlinson produced his pioneering email work. At the time, network links from one address to another were highly unreliable, often overloaded or simply unavailable. SMTP offered as a remedy a store-and-forward design that enabled one SMTP gateway server to transmit a message to another server, which would accept, store and ultimately transfer (or hop) the message to a closer relay for delivery. When SMTP gateways are operating in relay mode, the receiving mail server will see only the IP address of the "last hop" SMTP relay. Since the envelope and header addressing information are just text, they can be easily manipulated and forged. Therefore, when an SMTP gateway is operating in relay mode, the true nature of the sender is easily masked, because neither the headers nor the IP address of the sender can be verified.

In traditional mail, the end result would be a package arriving on a doorstep without a recognizable or traceable indication of its source. A suspicious recipient would likely reject this sort of delivery. The IP address of the SMTP gateway that delivered the message to its final destination is the only information that can be identified with certainty, and that goes to the heart of the problem with today's email transfer protocol.

Email messages may be transmitted from random, intermediate servers with their own IP addresses, giving nefarious emailers the ability to send fraudulent mail through presumably innocent mail relays with no trace of their true identity. While this weakness is improving with technology advances, the anonymity of SMTP remains an ongoing challenge. This relay function still remains an integral component of SMTP.

The Next Hop

The Internet's evolution over the years has made links much more reliable, eliminating the need to relay mail through multiple hops. As a result, a sending SMTP gateway typically connects directly to a receiver's SMTP gateway. The vast majority of SMTP gateways today will reject requests to relay mail on behalf of another sender because such requests are often for illicit purposes. Nevertheless, the relay function remains an integral component of SMTP, and IT administrators occasionally will forget to turn it off. This creates an open relay that illegitimate mailers can use to mask their identities. Attempts to automatically identify and notify legitimate operators of open relays have proven effective at securing email infrastructure, although outbreaks of such massive viruses as the recent *SoBig* bug still manage to infect millions of machines, enabling PCs to be hijacked and masking the IP addresses of "criminal" mailers.

DEFINITION: HOP

A hop is the journey from one SMTP relay to another. Today's email messages typically take one hop to cross the Internet; a few years ago it could take as many as 20 hops.

Email Abuse Threatens Legitimate Email

SMTP has changed very little over time. Its strength remains in its simplicity and universal acceptance, although SMTP's inability to consistently trace email sender identity remains a serious shortcoming. This lack of accountability has led to the proliferation of email abuse, which threatens to undermine the entire medium. In response, IT administrators and Internet Service Providers are applying increasingly sophisticated, costly filtering systems at their own incoming SMTP gateways. The increasing intelligence deployed at these gateways reflects the importance of distinguishing legitimate from illegitimate email, and the need to provide email with the type of secure environment that can help email fulfill its revolutionary promise.

QUICK LOOK

EMAIL 101

SMTP Is the Email Protocol

A message store such as Microsoft Exchange will generate an email and hand it to the SMTP gateway (or relay). The gateway queues messages, looks up the IP address of the receiver and then delivers the message using the SMTP protocol.

Envelope Address vs. Header Address

Like a traditional letter, an email has an envelope from and to address. These addresses are used by the mail server to route mail. The headers from and to are the addresses that appear in the client software, such as Microsoft Outlook.

SMTP Gateways Can "Relay" Messages

As mentioned earlier, email is a store and forward medium. So an SMTP gateway can temporarily accept an email, and then send it on to another SMTP server closer to the destination address. Today this practice is rarely used, but it remains a technique used to send spam.

IP Address Is Currently the Only Form of Identity

Since envelope and header addresses are easily forged, all that can be authenticated about a given email is the IP address of the last gateway server that sent it.

"I don't think **CAN** Spam will have much impact on the spammers who are already breaking the law, and I don't believe it can solve the really bad problems out there. The only solution will be technology that can track down disreputable spammers' identities so that they can be prosecuted."

JOSH BAER
Founder and Chief Executive Officer,
SKYLIST Inc.

2

SPAM EPIDEMIC
ITS ROOTS CAN BE TRACED TO THE VIKINGS.
SORT OF.

A ccording to accepted Internet lore, spam owes its identity to a comedy skit from the old Monty Python show in which a group of rowdy Norsemen, inspired by a passion for canned meat, drowns out a couple's attempts to order a meal with repeated chants of "Spam! Spam! Lovely Spam!" The beleguered restaurant goers' ultimate frustration has been widely adopted as a metaphor for the current tide of unsolicited commercial email that is flooding email servers and user inboxes.

FAST FACT:
Spam costs American corporations between $10 billion and $87 billion per year.

Yet spam's meteoric rise over the last few years is no laughing matter. Its dominance on the Internet places it in the pantheon of such great American nuisances as junk mail and telemarketing. While spam's proliferation reflects the ubiquity of email, it also underscores the unique vulnerability of existing email protocol to fraudulent, offensive or just plain annoying electronic pitches from unrecognized or masquerading sources.

Spam Growth

Recent studies indicate that the growth of spam is not only trying emailers' patience, but also threatening the credibility of the medium itself. An October 2003 report from the *Pew Internet & American Life Project* reports that 70 percent of 1,380 surveyed Internet users said spam has made being online "unpleasant or annoying," while 52 percent of respondents claimed spam has made them "less trusting of email in general." Thirty percent indicated they are concerned their filtering devices may be blocking legitimate incoming mail, while more than 20 percent said they fear their mail is being blocked before reaching its destination.

It's estimated that more than 30 billion emails circulate via the Internet daily, with spam accounting for more than 70 percent of that volume. Low-cost bulk mailings hawk everything from get-rich-quick opportunities to cures for impotence, and with enough recipients responding at least once, the money made ensures that spam will remain a growth industry, at least for the near term. Although many commercial emailers are actually selling legitimate products or services, some are profiting from illicitly harvesting and selling email addresses gleaned through bogus solicitations. Others are virtually hijacking recipients' PCs via placement of viruses that can turn a recipient into an unsuspecting conduit for enormous bulk email blitzes. A November 24, 2003, *Newsweek* report refers to such victims as "spam zombies," and notes that university students are particularly vulnerable, given their access to their schools' high-speed, state-of-the-art computing networks.

While spam may be a greater headache for personal users, who typically lack the advanced screening systems deployed by businesses, the battle to stanch its spread is hitting the corporate world where it counts most: the bottom line.

The Pew study reports wide-ranging estimates on what businesses spend combating spam— from (US) $50 to (US) $1,400 per worker, per year, with an overall annual cost to American corporations in direct expenses and lost productivity at between (US) $10 billion and (US) $87 billion.

Introducing the Nano-cent

Unsolicited bulk mail has long been a cornerstone of the traditional postal system. And yet the delivery of "Val-Pack Coupons" or credit card offers in our mailboxes doesn't evoke the emotional and widespread consumer outrage that spam does. This is because the cost of traditional mailings keeps the volume of mail offers we receive at an acceptable, if somewhat annoying, level. A typical direct mail piece might cost (US) $2 to produce and distribute, with an open rate of less than 1 percent. And yet this cost/benefit ratio is compelling enough for certain marketers to pursue. The cost of an email marketing piece can be as low as a nano-cent, or 1/100 of a millionth of a cent. Imagine how many "val-packs" we'd get at this price. This is the economic engine behind spam.

Efforts to Control Spam Growth

Such compelling economics and the correspondingly large, imprecise growth estimates reflect the recent explosion of spam and the uncertainty over how to control it. Public and private sector officials are racing to catch up, and, in the process, confronting the many issues that spam raises, including free speech —a cornerstone of the Internet—privacy protection and the long-term impact on legitimate e-commerce.

Among the Biggest Hurdles Is Defining Spam

Most would agree with the description of spam as unsolicited email from an unknown sender. Yet a one-size-fits-all definition cannot account for all unsolicited messages, many of which are sent with legitimate intentions and welcomed, or at least tolerated, by recipients.

Business and government leaders are weighing in with increasingly sophisticated software filters and new legislation, yet the holes in their nets remain too wide to eliminate the problem altogether. Smart spammers mask their identities and intent, and can easily circumvent legal restrictions by hopping effortlessly offshore, or cover their tracks by continuously shifting their Internet locations.

FAST FACT
The CAN Spam Act of 2003 preempts a growing collection of inconsistent state laws.

"The problem," says an attorney specializing in privacy protection, "is with enforcement. Violations are very difficult to trace, and there just aren't the resources available to pursue such cases."

Legislation to the Rescue?
The CAN Spam Act of 2003

New federal guidelines, billed in the media as "landmark legislation," were recently signed into law as the CAN Spam Act of 2003. It creates the first national standards for sending commercial email and wireless solicitations, while placing enforcement with the Federal Trade Commission, which has historically pursued spam violations under provisions of the FTC Act.

"This clearly gives us some new tools," said an FTC attorney. "But we've said all along that this is no silver bullet in the fight against spam."

CAN Spam protects email marketers' rights to send messages, provided their messages contain opt-out mechanisms that permit recipients to get off the sender's mail list. The law forbids the transfer or sale of a recipient's address acquired through the opt-out mechanism. In addition, CAN Spam mandates inclusion of a working return email address, a clear indication that the message is an advertisement, as well as the sender's real, physical address in the body of the message.

The law also subjects to penalty any business that is knowingly promoted in an unsolicited commercial email that contains false or misleading header information, even if the spammer who initiated the email cannot be identified. Under CAN Spam, spammers can face civil penalties for acquiring multiple email addresses by automated means to circulate unsolicited commercial email. However, by constantly shifting addresses, spammers are difficult to track down, and their messages become hard to filter.

Other Anti-Spam Efforts

Legislation also requires that the FTC generate future reports on other proposed solutions to spam, including the institution of a do-not-call registry, similar to the list for telemarketing. The FTC is charged with developing a plan for the creation of such a list, or providing a compelling argument why launching such a list is not possible. The FTC will also spearhead creation of subject-line labeling requirements.

"CAN Spam provides a good framework for legitimate Internet marketers, but isn't likely to change the behavior of spammers who are in the business of identity theft, address harvesting or other types of email scams," says Josh Baer, founder and chief executive officer of SKYLIST Inc., an Austin, Texas-based provider of email marketing software and hosting services.

"The law certainly helps clarify what the rules are, and provides commercial emailers with a checklist of what's appropriate," Baer continues "But it's really only relevant to those emailers who are concerned with doing the right thing. It will help the good companies have a better understanding of what's right and wrong."

Federal vs. State Law

CAN Spam preempts anti-spam legislation now on the books in 37 states. The federal and state regulations share many similarities. According to the National Conference of State Legislatures, the state laws generally prohibit the falsification or misrepresentation of a message's origin, use of a third-party Internet address without permission and inclusion of false or misleading information in a message's subject line. Other common requirements call for the inclusion of a valid toll-free telephone number or email address, enabling recipients to opt-out of future e-mail messages, as well as placement of labeling in the subject line indicating whether the message features advertising or adult content; i.e. ADV or ADV:ADLT.

California's anti-spam law is widely regarded as one of the nation's toughest. Among its components is a ban on unsolicited commercial email in which the sender does not have a pre-existing relationship with the recipient, and applies to messages sent from California or to Californians. The law also gives email recipients the right to sue on a capped, per-message basis. Lauded by many for its aggressive stance on spam, the legislation's broad scope has also been criticized as a catalyst for frivolous litigation that would hinder operations of legitimate commercial emailers.

The Filter Front

As government enforcers pursue legal remedies,

industry has been at work developing new lines of defense against spam, namely filtering technologies designed to identify and discard spam before it reaches recipients. Internet service providers such as Microsoft and AOL are leading the fight. According to the 2003 *Pew Internet & American Life Project* report, the companies estimate daily receipt of about 2.4 billion spam messages a day. AOL says it is blocking up to 80 percent of the messages that hit its servers on a daily basis, which translates to an estimated 67 messages per inbox each day. The spam deluge is taxing server storage, bandwidth, administrators and programmers. The collateral damage—aside from overall consumer frustration with the spam that does get through—includes those innocent messages that are inadvertently blocked.

FAST FACT:
Microsoft and AOL estimate they receive about 2.4 billion spam messages a day.

How We Weed Out Spam

Anti-spam technology applies a range of constantly evolving strategies to weed out unwanted email. The most effective systems use real-time updates to stay ahead of spammer tactics. Less sophisticated systems use static rules that may be effective when first deployed, but will degrade over time as spammers adapt. All systems contain one or many variants of the following basic techniques.

Blacklists Blacklists or databases of known spammer addresses are used to instantly cross-check at the gateway server.

White-lists White-lists are registries of known or trusted senders. The largest and most innovative white-list is Bonded Sender. Bonded Sender requires a legitimate sender to post a financial bond. If end-users complain about spam from a bonded sender, the bond can be debited. This system is effective because it changes the fundamental economics that drive spam.

Filters Content filtering, which relies on increasingly complex algorithms to search out select words and phrases, helps identify messages as spam.

Image-Based Systems Image-based systems determine whether an email's digital ID code shows up repeatedly in other places on the Internet. If it does, then it is likely bulk spam.

Challenge/Response The sender must reply to a question or "challenge" before mail will be accepted. Computer-generated spam is unable to respond to challenges. This system has a major impact on end-user behavior and thus has limited acceptance.

Where Do We Go From Here?

As spammers adapt to anti-spam hurdles, technology is attempting to keep pace. One such service requires unknown senders to type in a printed code before transmitting their message. Computer-generated spam is unable to comply, and is effectively blocked at the source. Other solutions are aimed at protecting legitimate senders, including an evolving new network that financially bonds commercial emailers, placing them on a database of approved senders. These and other remedies to the spreading spam crisis are detailed in Part III.

QUICK LOOK

Spamming Is Good Business
A traditional direct mail piece can cost about (US) $2.00. A commercial email can be less than 1/100 of a millionth of a cent. When mailing is "almost free", even shoddy, uncompelling offers can yield financial returns. The trick is avoiding the filters and getting mail through.

Legislation Isn't the Answer
The recent CAN Spam Act is a useful tool, but won't stop spam on its own. Enforcement is difficult and definitions are tricky.

Filtering is a Cat and Mouse Game
As companies come up with new filter algorithms, spammers find ways around them. The best filters update in near-real time.

"With the really
good viruses, people
don't even know they're
being attacked."

RICHI JENNINGS

Lead Analyst,

Ferris Research's Spam and Boundary Services Practice

3

THE VIRUS PREDICAMENT
FROM THE BRAIN, TO MY DOOM,
I LOVE YOU, MELISSA.

Their names incorporate a host of literary genres, from romance (*I Love You*) to horror (*My Doom*), yet their intent is universal: to annoy, disrupt and otherwise wreak havoc for unsuspecting computer users.

Computer viruses and their e-cousins—worms, Trojan horses and even spyware—have evolved over the last two decades as serious threats to security in the computer/Internet age. They can be harmless, causing random displays of silly messages or temporary, erratic computer performance. Or they can be devastating, stealing sensitive information, wiping out files and erasing hard drives. Whether created by thrill-seeking teen vandals, zealous hack-tivists or profit-hungry spammers, the fertile field of electronic infections underscores the insecurity of today's computing environment. Sophisticated new technologies have mounted a vigorous defense, yet the attackers continue to adapt their arsenals and exploit even the smallest security cracks.

Computer Virus Definitions and Evolution

Broadly defined, computer viruses are chunks of parasitic software code that propagate each time an infected program is run, damaging or destroying other files and programs on the same computer. With human aid, intentional or inadvertent, viruses spread to and infect other computers just as biological viruses are passed between human carriers. Over the years, viruses have evolved to capitalize on expanding transmission vectors. In keeping with the biological lexicon often applied to computer attacks, the term *vector* is borrowed from the medical reference to a viral transmission environment. A common cold vector, for example, could be a handshake, where an infected person spreads his illness to a friend, who unknowingly infects

FAST FACT:
Modern virus defenses reflect their biological brethren. Outbreak filters control and quarantine traffic— similar to the Centers for Disease Control. Image filters identify and destroy infected traffic— similar to a vaccine.

himself after the handshake by rubbing his eye or touching his lips.

A History

The first documented PC virus, *The Brain*, was written in Pakistan and launched in 1986. Such early infections were typically the result of *floppy swaps* with viruses jumping from computer to computer via infected disks. Once downloaded from the disk, the virus attacked from its hiding spot within the executable carrier program. Others viruses were hidden in disks' boot sectors, and activated when the host computer was turned on, or "booted up." Today's widespread adoption of more secure compact discs and the spread of downloadable, web-based programming have greatly reduced the threat of floppy swap infection, forcing virus code writers to adapt to new computing terrain.

The current infection vector is primarily Internet based with emails transporting viruses in executable attachments. Viruses and related threats can also be hidden in address extensions to exploit bugs in the client or mail

servers, or to smash through server buffers and
dump their infected code.

Email-Borne Viruses

Dramatic examples of the power of email-borne
viruses include *Melissa*, which

emerged as the fastest-
spreading virus on record by
replicating itself through
Microsoft Word documents
sent by email. Victims downloaded the document and
launched the virus, which
then latched onto the first 50 names in the victim's Outlook address book. Because the messages
appeared to originate from a recognized address,
unsuspecting readers had no qualms about opening it. The more recent *I Love You* virus carried
its infected code as an executable attachment,
which when launched damaged files and copied
itself to everyone in the victim's address book. *I
Love You* worked more as a Trojan horse attack,
which is defined on the following page.

"These reflect a whole new class of attacks

designed to exploit the new Internet vectors," said Richi Jennings, a research analyst with Ferris Research, a marketing and technology research firm specializing in messaging and digital communications.

Malware

Viruses are part of what are commonly referred to as "malware," which includes worms, Trojan horses and spyware.

Worms are opportunistic programs engineered to move about in search of security holes in software or operating systems. Once inside, the worm replicates itself quickly to infiltrate other machines throughout a computer network. Worms are not designed for data destruction, but can have a damaging effect by overwhelming and slowing down victims' systems. Firewalls are the most effective prevention for worms.

Trojan horses, like the name implies, are programs disguised as something desirable, but that actually perform something terrible, such as, erasing a hard drive. Trojan horses do not replicate themselves.

Spyware often comes packaged as part of some

ostensibly legitimate software. Once downloaded and run, it spies on its host's Internet habits. Hackers may use spyware to steal credit card numbers or other sensitive data, or to collect information for use in illicit marketing.

On the Attack!

The motivation behind e-attacks, like the attacks themselves, has mutated over time. Initial attacks were often credited to computer geek show-offs, including part-time hackers out to prove their technological prowess. "Peer recognition was and remains a strong motivator for a lot of virus writers," Jennings said. "Unfortunately for them, it often leads to their downfall."

Other attacks, particularly ones that modify a company's website, are often traced to politically motivated "hack-tivism," which relies on the popularity of the Internet to attack its targets. The more sinister assaults, however, are carried out for commercial gain, including viruses that exploit open mail relays to steal private information, spread spam, or even force their way via the Internet onto an unprotected computer to hijack it for use as a zombie spam distributor. What's most troubling is that many victims remain unaware that their computer has been taken over. "Good virus writers don't want you to know what's happening," Jennings said.

FAST FACT

The Brain, an early computer virus, took months to propagate. Modern viruses such as *Melissa* propagate globally in two to three hours.

Anti-Virus Software

The question remains whether viruses and related malware will become more problematic, and whether they can be wiped out altogether in the coming years. A new industry of anti-virus software has emerged to ward off many types of attack, yet the problem persists as virus programmers adapt to the challenges.

Virus Writers Rise to the Challenge

Virtual networks of virus writers share ideas and techniques for getting around firewalls and exploiting weaknesses.

"Nowadays, if you get into the right crowd, you can essentially download a virus-writing kit and launch your own attack," Jennings said. "It may not be very good, but there are still enough unprotected systems out there that are susceptible. The trick is to make people aware of the importance of firewalls, and other anti-virus technologies, and of the various tricks employed to get at their systems."

Email forgery and the creation of bogus websites, for example, have emerged as fertile attack vectors, trapping unsuspecting computer users. Even the most sophisticated networks can get nailed, despite their attention to security. An intercompany network can be airtight, but if an employee takes his laptop home, plugs into his personal Internet connection and unwittingly contracts a virus, he can easily expose the entire corporate network to infection the following day when he logs back in.

The Best Defense—Tips From Industry Experts

By following this checklist, you can help lessen or stop viruses and other related threats.

- **Anti-Virus Software**
  Install and regularly update anti-virus scanning software to keep ahead of the thousands of new viruses that are discovered each year.

- **Keep Up To Date With Patches**
  Keep operating systems, email programs and

web browsers up to date by downloading
recommended patches.

♠ Firewall
Install a firewall if you do not already have one.

♠ Be Vigilant
Don't open email or email attachments from
unknown sources.

Don't open attachments to emails with strange or
unanticipated subject lines.

Don't open unexpected email attachments from
known sources. It's possible their address is
being used to transport an infected attachment
without their knowledge. To be safe, call to
confirm the indicated source actually sent it.

Never download a file or a program sent from an
unknown source, or from the Internet, unless you
are sure the source is credible. Scan all programs
with anti-virus software before running them.

♠ Check Floppy Drive
Eliminate boot sector viruses by removing
floppy disks from disk drives before starting
your computer.

✉ Online Email Posting

Avoid posting email online. If necessary, replace the "@"symbol with an "A" to foil automated spam harvesters.

✉ Back It Up

Back files up regularly to minimize the impact of an attack.

✉ Check Your Settings

Make certain the Macro Virus Protection function is enabled on all Microsoft applications, and think twice about opening non-data files, executable email attachments that contain such extensions as EXE or COM.

Keep Current

The best defense against viruses in the future is education. Even the most sophisticated IT departments struggle to keep messaging safe. By implementing the newest technology advancements and staying current, virus epidemics, like their biological counterparts, can be controlled and, perhaps one day, eliminated completely.

QUICK LOOK

THE VIRUS PREDICAMENT

Outbreaks Happen Rapidly

The first viruses took months to propagate. Modern viruses spread globally in a few hours.

Defense In Depth

Most companies deploy a multi-vendor, multi-layer strategy. Overlapping anti-virus vendors ensures maximum protection and minimum reaction time.

Containment Is Key

The cost of virus cleanup can exceed (US) $100 per seat. New technologies that can proactively block viruses as they emerge appear highly promising.

Part II

EMAIL: RULES, REGULATIONS AND LIABILITIES.

"We believe that spam is one of the most significant threats to the future development of the Internet. There is consensus in our industry that spam is an ever-growing problem that needs to be eradicated not just to protect consumers, but brands and business as well."

H. ROBERT WIENTZEN
President and CEO, Direct Marketing Association

4

EMAIL MARKETING STANDARDS
A LITTLE SELF-REGULATION GOES A LONG WAY.

While CAN Spam (see Chapter 2) offers a useful outline on how to avoid legal prosecution, commercial marketers are still advised to adhere to the collection of best practices adopted by the industry that will not only help them follow the law, but also keep their mail from being inadvertently labeled as spam, or dismissed by potential customers.

Self-Regulation as a Response to Spam

The American Association of Advertising Agencies (AAAA), the Association of National Advertisers (ANA) and the Direct Marketing Association (DMA) are three of the largest trade groups representing advertisers and marketers. Together in October 2003 they released a joint set of self-regulating guidelines designed to promote and defend legitimate email marketing. The rules were released prior to the passage of The CAN Spam Act of 2003, but remain adopted principles of the associations, according to the ANA.

The AAAA, ANA and DMA adopted the following principles as a way to distinguish themselves from spammers. By complying with this list, you will be well on your way to becoming a "legitimate" email marketer.

- **The Subject Line**
  The subject line of an email must be honest and not misleading or deceptive.

- **The Return Address**
  A valid return email address and the physical address of the sender should be clearly identified. Marketers are encouraged to use their company or brand names in their domain address and prominently throughout the message.

- **The Sender**
  An email should clearly identify the sender and the subject matter at the beginning of the email.

- **List Removal Option**
  All commercial email (except for billing purposes) must provide consumers with a clear and

conspicuous electronic option to be removed from lists for future email messages from the sender. The removal process must be easy to find and easy to use.

✉ Opt-Out Option

If a company sending commercial email has multiple distinct brands or affiliates, notice and opt-out should be provided based on the likely perspective of the average consumer. Each separate brand or affiliate, as the consumer is likely to perceive it, must offer notice and a process for removal from marketing lists in all commercial email (except for billing purposes).

✉ Email Address Acquisitions

Marketers should not acquire email addresses surreptitiously through automated mechanisms (such as robots or spiders) without the consumer/customer's informed consent. This includes a prohibition on dictionary attacks or other mechanisms for fabricating email addresses without providing notice and choice to the consumer.

✉ Honor Remove Requests

"Remove" means "remove." The electronic remove feature must be reliable, functional and prompt.

✉ Third Parties

Email lists must not be sold or provided to unre-lated third parties, unless the owner of the list has provided notice, and the ability to be removed from such transfer to each email address on the list. Related third parties are defined as brands/subsidiaries within the same parent company, as well as outside affinity partners, as a reasonable consumer is likely to perceive them.

✉ Privacy Policy

A commercial email should contain the sender's privacy policy, either within the body of the email or via a link.

Consumer Tune-Out at Peak

In statements accompanying the release of the guidelines, Bob Liodice, president and CEO of the ANA said, "Right now, 'consumer tune-out' with various forms of advertising and communication is at its peak. In particular, there is substantial con-sumer push-back with spam. Our members—the nation's leading advertisers and marketers—are concerned that spam is killing the potential and promise of email marketing. With these principles, we are asking corporate marketers to abide by tough marketing guidelines so that consumers can easily differentiate between legitimate email marketing messages and spam."

Stamping Out Spam

By adding their own solution into the mix, members of the AAAA, ANA and DMA joined other efforts, such as technical innovations and federal legislation, to stamp out spam. The incredible amount of spam generated daily is hurting legitimate companies who use email as a marketing tool. In the hopes of elevating legitimate, responsible and consumer-friendly businesses, the associations' stringent set of self-regulatory principles also aim to prove to consumers that not all email offers should be viewed suspiciously.

For More Information

**The American Association of
Advertising Agencies (AAAA)**
www.aaaa.org

The Association of National Advertisers (ANA)
www.ana.net

Direct Marketing Association (DMA)
www.the-dma.org

QUICK LOOK

EMAIL MARKETING STANDARDS

Email Marketing Is Powerful

With its ability to target at the individual level, email marketing often has response rates that are 10x greater than traditional direct mail, at 1/100th the cost.

Spam Is Spoiling the Party

The rapid growth of spam is eroding consumer trust and causing them to "tune out."

Use Common Sense

Make sure subject lines are clear, unsubscribes work and lists are managed carefully.

CAN-Spam Makes Advertisers Responsible

If you are a consumer brand and you obtain a list from a third-party affiliate, you are responsible for managing and maintaining unsubscribe requests. You are also liable for CAN Spam violations.

"Enterprises today are struggling to deal with a complex regulatory environment full of costly, unfunded mandates, while still managing tight budgets. Implementing compliance architecture with an enterprise's current technology can help reduce the cost of regulatory compliance. Businesses need to use technologies that eliminate requirements to hire external auditors or consultants every time a new law appears."

RICH MOGULL
Director, Gartner Research

5

RULES, REGULATIONS AND HEADACHES
KEEPING COMPLIANT IN INFORMATION PRIVACY, SECURITY AND RETENTION.

L ong regarded as hearsay, akin to idle water-cooler conversation, email content is gaining popularity as a tool for litigators and government regulators scouring for corporate missteps or non-compliance. With the enormous volumes of email coursing into, through and out of even the smallest businesses, regulation adherence demands expert email management and awareness of its many pitfalls. For corporate communication, "email is the first place people go to these days," notes an information technology analyst. "And that information is increasingly expected to be managed and documented. It's what legislators (and regulators) are looking for."

Privacy and Security Standards

The list of regulations that affect email use and management run the professional gamut from Wall Street to the local doctor's office. Standards for the application and documentation of e-traffic are included—directly and indirectly—in a host of government mandates, each addressing issues of information privacy, security and retention.

Ben L. Littauer, an independent consultant specializing in Internet and communications technologies, noted in a recent Ferris Research webinar, that maintaining effective privacy and security standards is more critical than ever given the expanding scope of the regulatory environment.

Littauer characterizes privacy issues as those matters relating to policies and procedures for handling an individual's or client's information, including financial and medical data. Security issues, meanwhile, relate to specific technical methods deployed to protect electronic data from theft or tampering. Distinguishing between the two, and successfully addressing their requirements for compliance, demands a more rigorous approach to electronic information management— including email use and storage—than simply installing security software or hardware.

FAST FACT: Regulation adherence demands expert email management and awareness of its many pitfalls.

Regulation Compliance: The Challenge

To successfully navigate today's regulatory briar patch, businesses are compelled to educate themselves on the requirements, keep pace with technological applications and monitor industry best practices. Comprehensive privacy and security solutions cannot be "bought off the shelf," Littauer said. "The bottom line: Beware of easy (solutions). You really have to understand where the holes are."

How HIPAA Affects Email Management

The Health Insurance Portability and Accountability Act (HIPAA) was passed in 1996 to help people acquire or maintain health insurance between jobs, even if they have a serious health condition. Administrative simplification is a prime

HIPAA objective, and is based on a set of electronic healthcare codes, privacy and confidentiality requirements for handling personal health information (PHI), as well as security standards for safeguarding that information whether shared in written, verbal or electronic form, including email, between healthcare institutions and professionals.

FAST FACT:
HIPAA stands for the Health Insurance Portability and Accountability Act, and was passed in 1996.

HIPAA's Privacy Rule

The Privacy Rule, a key component of HIPAA, was issued by the U.S. Department of Health and Human Services to protect the use and disclosure of individuals' health information, while providing for the efficient flow of information required for quality healthcare delivery.

Complexities in the Privacy Rule, which took effect in April 2003, require careful analysis and application. Language pertaining to individually "created or received" information, for example, stipulates that information transmitted by a patient to a healthcare professional or agency is not covered, yet once that data is received, and passed on in any way by the recipient, it falls under HIPAA protections.

HIPAA's Security Rule

The Security Rule is slated to take effect on April 21, 2005. It sets standards for the implementation of technical security measures to guard against unauthorized access to protected health information that is stored or transmitted over an electronic communications network. Requirements on how security is implemented are unspecific, yet an effective method is required to be in place that includes integrity controls to ensure that electronically transmitted health information is not modified without detection at any time prior to its ultimate disposal. It also stipulates that information be encrypted when deemed appropriate. Integrity controls and encryption are both considered "addressable" issues under the rule, which means that healthcare professionals or agencies must provide a strong reason if they choose not to apply them to certain types of health information.

Survey Reveals HIPAA Compliance Shortfall

HIPAA compliance is critical, yet a Phoenix Health Systems and Healthcare Information and

Management Systems Society survey indicates the healthcare industry has far to go in meeting its mandated responsibilities.

For example, of the 428 healthcare organizations responding to their Fall 2003 questionnaire:

* 12 to 27 percent of the organizations (sorted by categories, including providers, payers, etc.), reported they were not in compliance with the Privacy Rule.

* Roughly one-half of all respondents reported that their organizations had experienced at least one privacy breach in the preceding six months.

* And on the security front, nearly one-half of all participating organizations reported they would not be compliant with the HIPAA Security Rule by the April 2005 deadline.

More Regulations and Information Management

Here are a few more examples of how federal regulations are impacting email management:

The Gramm-Leach-Bliley Act The Gramm-Leach-Bliley (GLBA) Act was enacted in 1999 to repeal 1930s legislation that prohibited banks, securities firms and insurance companies from affiliating. Under the act, such entities may affiliate within a new financial holding company (FHC) structure to provide one-stop shopping for financial services. GLBA's definition of financial institution includes banks, credit unions, securities dealers, insurance companies, mortgage brokers/lenders, financial planners, credit card companies and real estate appraisers.

Among GLBA's many provisions, are privacy guidelines, which according to a summary from the Securities Industry Association, require that all financial institutions, regardless of whether they form an FHC, disclose to customers their policies and practices for protecting the privacy of personal information. This disclosure must give customers the ability to opt-out of information sharing arrangements with unaffiliated third parties. GLBA, however, allows financial institutions to share customers' personal information with their corporate affiliates without consumer consent.

> **FAST FACT:**
> Public companies that do not adopt a compliance management architecture will spend 50 percent more annually to achieve Sarbanes-Oxley compliance.

The SEC The Securities and Exchange Commission (SEC) and the National Association of Securities

Dealers have an email maintenance policy, which requires brokerages to review and retain records, and have systems in place for easy access to documents for regulatory review. In recent years, the SEC has actively pursued organizations that have not complied.

The Sarbanes-Oxley Act

The Sarbanes-Oxley Act, passed in 2002, in the wake of the highly publicized Enron and WorldCom financial scandals, is designed to protect shareholders and the general public from accounting errors and fraudulent reporting by publicly held companies. Administered by the Securities and Exchange Commission, the act dictates which business records are to be stored and for how long, affecting not only companies' financial operations, but also their IT departments, which are charged with managing and archiving electronic data. The legislation requires that all business records, including pertinent electronic records and messages, must be saved for at least five years.

In a March 2004 statement released during the *Gartner Symposium/ITxpo 2004*, Gartner Inc., a provider of research and analysis on the global information technology industry, predicts, "public companies that do not adopt compliance management architecture will spend 50 percent more annually to achieve Sarbanes-Oxley compliance." The Gartner release, however, warned against "vendor hype" that suggests a wide range of technologies is the solution to compliance with Sarbanes-Oxley, noting that many organizations already have many of the software tools required. The organization added that companies with good security, business continuity planning, as well as document and business process management systems currently in place have a solid foundation for their compliance architecture.

FAST FACT: In April 2005 HIPAA's Security Rule is slated to take effect and requires implementation of technical security measures to guard against unauthorized access to protected healthcare information.

"By expanding and standardizing the use of those systems, adding some business intelligence and perhaps a compliance tool for reporting, an organization can rapidly deploy a Level 1 architecture," said Rich Mogull, Director, Gartner Research.

Regulatory Compliance

The federal regulatory list goes on, including comprehensive requirements from the Food and Drug Administration, the Internal Revenue Service, and insurance industry overseers. High-profile corporate scandals in recent years have contributed to email's rising stature as fair game—indeed, a discovery target of choice for litigators, regulators and auditors—reinforcing, that "an ounce of information management planning is worth its weight in gold," as noted by author Nancy Flynn in *E-Mail Rules (AMACOM Books, 2003).*

Regulatory compliance demands action,
namely the implementation of
a document management system that identifies
and processes key correspondence.

"It's not about saving all email. It's about identifying the essential parts of the organization and what they are communicating from the CIO, CEO and CFO to the auditors and attorneys," said an information technology analyst at a Fortune 500 company, noting that in many of the new and developing regulations a primary focus is on promoting "access and transparency—(standards) we will likely see implemented over and over in markets around the world."

Regulations for email management will only grow as the medium continues to become more and more entrenched in every type of industry. It may seem impossible to be 100 percent compliant, but a proactive approach to understanding the rules and regulations will alleviate headaches later.

For More Information

The Health Insurance Portability and Accountability Act (HIPAA)
United States Department of Health and Human Services
http://aspe.hhs.gov/admnsimp/index.shtml

The Gramm-Leach-Bliley Act (GLBA)
United States Senate Committee on Banking,
Housing, and Urban Affairs
http://banking.senate.gov/conf/

The Sarbanes-Oxley Act
U.S. Securities and Exchange Commission
http://www.sec.gov/spotlight/sarbanes-oxley.htm

QUICK LOOK
RULES, REGULATIONS & HEADACHES

Email Is the Property of the Corporation
And as such, the corporation is responsible for its use. There is a huge amount of vendor hype on the market, but there is no substitute for management's understanding of the issues and proper planning.

HIPPA Matters for Some
Corporations in the healthcare industry must pay careful attention to the Health Insurance Portability and Accountability Act (HIPAA). It requires email encryption of sensitive patient information. This can be critical to implement.

GLBA Matters For Others
The Gramm-Leach-Bliley Act (GLBA) impacts the way financial institutions handle certain emails, and expands the definition of financial institution to include real estate appraisers and mortgage brokers.

"Whether you employ one part-time worker or 100,000 full-time professionals, any time you allow employees access to your email system, you put your assets, future and reputation at risk."

NANCY FLYNN
Executive Director, The ePolicy Institute

6

MANAGING THE COMPLEXITIES OF EMAIL
IT'S YOUR ASSETS ON THE LINE.

W hile spam continues to grab headlines in the email realm, it remains just one of many issues facing today's corporate email users. Email's positive impact on business efficiency is undeniable, but its widespread adoption in recent years continues to outpace its management. Many organizations are exposed to a variety of serious problems, ranging from lost productivity to a costly legal defense or penalties.

Effective Email Management

Spam's rapid growth has heightened awareness of the need to control what comes in and goes out of organizations' email networks. What often gets overlooked, however, is the enormous volume of internal messages, whose content can be damaging to a company's reputation and bottom line if a

FAST FACT:
A typical employee spends 25 percent of his or her workday on email.

plaintiff's attorney or regulatory agency subpoenas such correspondence. Effective email management demands careful attention on a variety of fronts, including message retention/deletion, the establishment of a comprehensive usage policy to provide well-defined parameters on acceptable practices and the technology to protect documents, and detect transgressions.

Whether it's circulation of offensive ("It was just supposed to be a joke!") adult material, an inter-office electronic exchange about a client account or company product, or the failure to efficiently produce specific email as part of legal discovery, the impact of a lax, poorly executed email policy can be devastating. Awareness of these challenges appears to be on the rise, although many organizations remain unresponsive to their new email management responsibilities.

Email Management Survey Results

Despite some progress, American business has far to go in the creation and enforcement of email policy, according to the findings of a "2003 E-Mail

Rules, Policies and Practices Survey" of 1,100 U.S. companies conducted by the American Management Association, The ePolicy Institute and Clearswift. The survey follows a similar canvas in 2001 conducted by the AMA and The ePolicy Institute and offers interesting data points, such as:

- 14 percent of respondents have been ordered by a court or regulatory agency to produce employee email, a five-point increase over the last two years.

- 90 percent of respondents say they send and receive personal email from work.

- A typical employee spends 25 percent of his or her work day on email.

- 52 percent of respondents monitor employee email, while 75 percent have a written email policy in place.

- 34 percent of respondents have a written email retention and deletion policy in place, but only 27 percent offer email retention/deletion training for employees.

- ♠ 48 percent of respondents offer e-policy education to employees, double the response from 2001.

- ♠ 40 percent of respondents use software to control written email content, with 23 percent combining that software with employee education.

- ♠ 90 percent of respondents have installed software to monitor incoming and outgoing mail, but only 19 percent use technology to monitor internal email.

- ♠ 86 percent of respondents say email has helped them work more efficiently, despite the fact that 92 percent say they receive spam mail at work.

In a statement accompanying the survey's release, Nancy Flynn, executive director of The ePolicy Institute, www.ePolicyInstitute.com, said

"Fortunately, by developing and implementing a strategic e-mail management program that combines rules, policy, education and enforcement, employers can anticipate e-mail disasters, address employee misuse, derail intentional abuse, curtail e-mail blunders and limit costly electronic liabilities."

Inside the Numbers

Flynn, co-author with Randolph Kahn, Esq., of *E-Mail Rules: A Business Guide to Managing Policies, Security and Legal Issues for E-Mail and Digital Communication* (AMACOM Books, 2003), said responses to the survey underscore the need for businesses to focus more intently on such email management imperatives as employee training and development of deletion and retention policies.

"In my opinion," Flynn said, "the results show that too many businesses are dropping the ball when it comes to the management of their email."

FAST FACT:
The Securities and Exchange Commission fined five prominent brokerage firms a combined (US) $8.3 million for failure to maintain adequate email records.

What You Don't Know Can Hurt You

Corporate America's failure to manage email messaging, particularly intra-company communication, points to a widespread lack of appreciation for the problems it can create. Based on the AMA/ePolicy Institute/Clearswift survey, the percentage of businesses actively archiving email through regular deletion and retention remains roughly the same as what was reported in the 2001 study.

Corporate America's lack of email management is surprising, Flynn said, given the number of high-profile legal and regulatory cases that have hinged on email and made headlines in the last two years. In each case, legal discovery of "smoking gun" email messages or inadequate email retention policies worked against the defendants.

In 2002, for example, the Securities and Exchange Commission fined five prominent brokerage firms a combined (US) $8.3 million for failure to maintain adequate email records. Further, the survey indicates that companies are increasingly called upon to produce their email records for review by government regulators, litigators or auditors, underscoring the growing need for businesses to take a more active approach to supervising their electronic communications.

"Email can be the electronic equivalent of DNA evidence in a legal case," Flynn said. "My bottom line is if you are giving workers access to your email system, and are not managing its use with effective policy and training, you're putting your business and its assets in jeopardy."

FAST FACT:
A company can be held responsible for its employees' wrongdoings, including email transgressions.

Managed E-Care

In *E-Mail Rules*, businesses are warned of the danger of "vicarious liability," which in legal parlance means that a company can be held responsible for its employees' wrongdoings, including email transgressions. Companies can minimize their legal exposure, the book reports, by establishing a comprehensive email policy that is supported by training and enforcement. Email policies not only educate employees about inadvertent risks they may be taking, but can also keep a business out of serious legal trouble by demonstrating to the courts or regulators that it is making a concerted effort to impose and enforce electronic communications standards throughout its organization.

Email Retention and Deletion Program

The centerpiece of any corporate email policy is the implementation of an effective email retention and deletion program, enabling businesses to access old emails that contain information pertinent to their operations with the speed and efficiency demanded by regulators, auditors and the courts.

In *E-Mail Rules*, Flynn notes that effective e-records management goes beyond mass archiving on back-up tapes. Such systems do not filter out non-essential, personal messages that can be damaging to a company's reputation if they are obtained through legal discovery, or provide for timely, efficient retrieval of specific correspondence. Flynn cites a development in the Enron case in which reams of employee emails, which had not been systematically stored or retrieved, were made public. Included were messages that had little bearing on the actual case, but contained personal, and often embarrassing information for employees.

With email's increasing use in legal discovery, businesses whose email traffic does not fall under regulatory retention guidelines should consider regular email purges, says a corporate IT specialist, who notes that many leading corporations purge their files on a monthly basis. While not advocated merely as a means to avoid legal problems, regular deletion policy should be practiced as a legitimate means to reduce the costs and hassles associated with back-up tape storage.

The challenge with purging, the IT manager notes, is that it's really effective only on the server side, and may not account for data already stored on an employee's laptop. For regulated industries such as healthcare and finance, document retention is mandated for defined periods, which, in turn, demands an effective archive management system to retrieve data efficiently.

FAST FACT:
Purging emails goes beyond what is stored on a server to what is on an employee's laptop or PC.

Thorough email retention and accessibility is especially critical for files that may relate to pending litigation. *E-Mail Rules* cites destruction of pertinent Enron files by accounting giant Arthur Andersen. Even though these files had not been subpoenaed at the time of their destruction, Andersen paid a heavy price for not having them available when investigators later requested them.

Protecting Your Assets

Email management is also critical for establishing content guidelines, promoting system security and protecting precious company data. While email plays a clear role in increased corporate productivity, it also provides fertile ground for information theft or loss, and virus attacks. At best, these problems can merely disrupt productivity. At worst, they can wreak long-term financial havoc. Imagine the devastating impact of sensitive product information or the details of an upcoming takeover bid trickling out to the competition, or the negative fallout for a hospital that inadvertently released protected patient information.

"A lot of problems are created unintentionally by employees who just don't know what's appropriate to send, download, delete or save," Flynn said. "Email management is a big job, and a lot of companies remain unaware (of its importance), or just don't take

it seriously until they're hit with a lawsuit.
By then, it may be too late."

Development of a strong usage policy, therefore, is essential to protect a company from potentially damaging email traffic. Delivering a powerful awareness campaign to make employees understand the potential risks of the messaging practices is the first step to avoiding such nightmare scenarios. Once absorbed, a comprehensive document classification system can be established to denote what messages are authorized to move beyond their intended target, or leave the company altogether. Once this classification system is in place, technology can be applied to protect documents from being shared inadvertently, and detect content problems with sophisticated scanning and filtering.

For More Information

E-mail Rules: A Business Guide to Managing Policies, Security, and Legal Issues For E-mail and Digital Communication

Nancy Flynn
The ePolicy Institute
nancy@epolicyinstitute.com
www.epolicyinstitute.com
614-451-3200

Randolph Kahn, ESQ.
Kahn Consulting, Inc.
Rkahn@kahnconsultingInc.com
www.kahnconsultingInc.com
847-266-0722

QUICK LOOK
MANAGING THE COMPLEXITIES OF EMAIL

Email Is the Smoking Gun
With increasing focus on email by regulators and attorneys, email is often the smoking gun. It is critical to have a clear email retention and deletion policy.

Archive Intelligently
Simply backing up old emails can create awkward situations where sensitive or personal employee information becomes public under subpoena. Deploy an archiving system that filters old emails and stores only relevant ones.

Deploy a "Goal Keeper"
Email filtering technology has matured to the point where it is easy to create fine-grained filters that run on the network perimeter. These filters can stop accidental or illicit distribution of intellectual property.

Train Your Team
Communicating clearly defined email usage guidelines is just as important as deploying technology to protect email. The best defense is a good offense.

Part III

EMAIL:
A MISSION-CRITICAL
FUTURE.

"Many organizations today are running outdated legacy SMTP relay implementations. To ensure business continuity for email services, we are strongly counseling clients to upgrade their mail relay infrastructures."

MATT CAIN
Senior Vice-President, Meta Group Inc.

7

SOUL OF A NEW EMAIL MACHINE
EVOLVING A UBIQUITOUS BUT DATED SYSTEM.

L ike a house built on a weak foundation, today's email system teeters on the brink of collapse. As noted throughout this book, email traffic has mushroomed in recent years, thanks in large part to the huge increase in illegitimate messaging. As a result, service providers and enterprises are scrambling to implement ad hoc solutions aimed at improving speed, efficiency and security. The combined weight of these incremental solutions placed atop existing infrastructure, however, jeopardizes the stability of the entire email system. Anyone who has suffered through an eight-hour email outage has undoubtedly gained an appreciation for the limitations and vulnerability of email's present infrastructure.

The vast majority of today's email gateway servers rely on technology developed more than 20 years ago, at a time when spam, viruses and related e-fraud were inconceivable.

As a result, the email marketplace faces
two alternatives:
brace for potential disaster, or start rebuilding
the system's inadequate foundation.

Email Weaknesses Revealed

Engineers at Hotmail were among the first to recognize cracks in email's foundation. Their early detection can be credited to the massive scale of their organization's operation, which magnified inherent weaknesses in the underlying email infrastructure. Launched by Jack Smith and Sabeer Bhatia, Hotmail pioneered the use of web-based email, utilizing hypertext markup language (HTML) for message body copy. HTML provided users with the revolutionary ability to embed attractive, reader-friendly fonts, graphics and images into their messages. Consumers loved it, but the format produced an enormous expansion of email throughput. In other words, a typical HTML email is about 10 times larger than a simple text email.

Hotmail's other breakthrough was the use of a web browser as a mail client. This enabled a free service that didn't require users to have a dedicated computer, or an Internet connection opening email up to huge segments of the population. The rapid adoption of Hotmail coupled with its 10 times larger messages put a huge strain on the existing email infrastructure.

FAST FACT
The company Hotmail created its name from the acronym HTML.

In response, Hotmail engineers identified the ideal characteristics for a next generation of email infrastructure.

The mail engine of the future, Hotmail engineers concluded, would deliver unprecedented concurrency to handle vast numbers of simultaneous connections, advanced queuing and very high throughput capacity to process incoming mail more efficiently. Such an engine would need to run 10 times faster than existing technologies, requiring a massive leap in processing power and a deep technological dive into the underlying computer operating system.

At the time, the Hotmail team could not justify such an intense investment in resources. The next generation machine, therefore, would have to wait for another company to develop and commercialize it.

Idea Lab Colleagues: An Extraordinary Meeting

As Hotmail's director of business development, Scott Weiss worked closely with CTO Jack Smith on developing and introducing new service features, gaining significant insights into the limitations of email's infrastructure along the way. Roughly a year after Microsoft's acquisition of Hotmail in 1999, Weiss left the organization to join Idea Lab, where he met Scott Banister, who brought his own, experience-based perspective on email infrastructure shortcomings to the table.

From ListBot to Idea Lab

As a University of Illinois freshman, Banister conceived ListBot, a novel corporate service that enabled any business with a website to communicate with customers via email newsletters. ListBot's runaway success soon forced the collegiate entrepreneur to shift his focus from campus activities to many of the same issues faced by

Smith, Weiss and the rest of the Hotmail team.

Shortly after selling ListBot—which was ultimately acquired by Microsoft, and remains in operation under the brand "bCentral," offering email hosting services for small and medium businesses—Banister teamed up with Idea Lab founder Bill Gross. Together, they created another Internet pillar—a pay-for-placement search engine that ultimately became Overture. This breakthrough idea earned Banister the somewhat esoteric title of "VP of Ideas" at Idea Lab.

Hops, Barley and a New Company

As Idea Lab colleagues, Weiss and Banister frequently enjoyed lunch at Stoddards, a popular brew-pub in nearby Sunnyvale, California. It was during one of these lunches (and a second round of beer) that Banister, Weiss and Smith reached the conclusion that a new company should be formed to rebuild email's cracking infrastructure. Together they launched IronPort Systems.

The New Foundation: IronPort's AsyncOS

Technical specialists at Hotmail and ListBot had concluded that the limitations of a traditional

UNIX-based gateway program rests not in the application itself, but in the way it interacts with the underlying operating system.

IronPort Systems has developed a unique operating system called AsyncOS, which is specifically engineered for the asynchronous processing of email messages.

Email is a connection-intensive medium. A decent-size enterprise may easily have thousands of simultaneous mail connec-tions coming in or going out. These connections are often relatively slow given that they may be connected to a busy mail server at the other end of the Internet. As a result, a traditional mail gateway often has difficulty processing a large number of simulta-neous connections. Most traditional email gateways

FAST FACT: AsyncOS comes from the term Asynchronous. Email is asynchronous, meaning messages can be processed in any order, the basis for the AsyncOS optimizations.

such as open-source Sendmail or Postfix are limited to 100 or, at most, 200 simultaneous connections simply because they cannot open enough threads to support additional connections. A thread is a portion of a computer's program that works independently, though in conjunction with other threads, to perform a larger task. In a traditional UNIX operating system, each thread of a program is allocated a fixed amount of memory with which to operate. Once all of the computer's memory is allocated, no new threads can be opened. A mail gateway program opens a new thread for every message it is sending or receiving at any given moment. Thus, in a traditional system, the operating system limits the number of messages that can be sent or received simultaneously.

Why AsyncOS Is Better

IronPort's AsyncOS features a "stackless" threading model that does not require a large memory stack for each thread. This enables the IronPort Gateway to support a massive concurrency of 10,000 simultaneous connections, which is 100 times greater than a traditional gateway.

> **FAST FACT:**
> A thread is a portion of a computer's program that works independently, though in conjunction with other threads to perform a larger task.

I/O Bottleneck Solved

This massive concurrency ensures that for all practical purposes the IronPort Gateway will never be connection bound. So, the IronPort Gateway will never give a busy signal to an incoming mail server. Solving the concurrency bottleneck means that the bottleneck shifts to the Input/Output (I/O) capability of the server. Since all messages in a gateway must be put on and off the system's hard disk, the gateway is an I/O-intensive application. The I/O bottleneck is addressed in AsyncOS in two ways: through IronPort's I/O-driven scheduler, and the AsyncOS file system.

How IronPort's AsyncOS Scheduler Works

AsyncOS takes advantage of the asynchronous nature of email to process messages in any order that is optimal. If a thread is actively using I/O, the system allows it to finish its I/O transaction, and will not incur the overhead of a context switch induced by a time-based scheduler. This increases the efficiency of the I/O system dramatically.

How IronPort's AsyncOS File System Works

Traditional gateways use the file system to maintain the state of the application. This means that each message is a unique file (or multiple files). The file system needs to keep track of where each of these millions of tiny files are located on disk. If a major receiving domain becomes unavailable and a queue starts to grow, the overhead associated with a traditional file system begins to drag down the machine's overall throughput. So, when the receiving mail domain comes back online, the gateway needs to resume delivery and clear the queue. But at the moment the gateway needs maximum throughput to clear the queue, the file system overhead actually minimizes throughput. So the queue grows, causing more overhead, which in turn results in a bigger queue. Eventually the system grinds to a halt, requiring administrator intervention.

FAST FACT
I/O is the Input/Output capability of a server. All messages in a gateway must be put on and off the system's hard disk, making an email gateway an I/O-intensive application.

FAST FACT
A single 2U IronPort appliance can replace 10 traditional UNIX servers, while cutting administrative time by 75%.

The AsyncOS file system is similar in nature to a high-performance journaling database. It is optimized for accessing large numbers of relatively small objects (messages) stored in its queue. The AsyncOS file system can manage very large queues, several weeks, worth of mail, and still experience less than 5 percent degradation in the throughput of the server.

A Better Email System

These optimizations are the result of more than 50 man-years of development and they lay the groundwork for a new infrastructure that is literally 10 times more powerful than existing legacy systems. IronPort's high-performance mail gateways have been deployed at the largest ISPs in the world, including AOL, RoadRunner and Bell Canada, as well as such large, global corporations as Dell, Viacom and Cisco Systems. This breakthrough in performance allows the system to perform much more sophisticated algorithms for securing incoming email.

QUICK LOOK
SOUL OF A NEW EMAIL MACHINE

Email Security Threats Strain the Gateway
Traditional UNIX-based email gateways are based on server architecture that dates back more than 20 years. Traditional gateways become overwhelmed with the flood of incoming spam and viruses.

The Limitation Is in the OS
The limitation of traditional email gateways lies in the interaction between the application and its underlying operating system.

Email Is Unique
Email is asynchronous, meaning messages can be processed in any order. This allows for massive optimizations. Email is also I/O intensive, since every message must run on and off the RAID subsystem.

The Next Generation Needs Its Own OS
The next-generation email infrastructure, such as that from IronPort Systems, requires its own operating system optimized for messaging application. A properly optimized OS will maximize concurrent email connections and efficiently manage I/O for maximum system throughput.

"As a leading source of online news, our business is dependent on email. Deliverability was our number one concern, and Bonded Sender ensures that our messages get delivered."

MARKUS MULLARKEY
Vice-President of Outbound Marketing Solutions, CNET

8

YOUR REPUTATION PRECEDES YOU

HOW SENDER REPUTATION CAN FIX EMAIL.

When the architecture of the current email infrastructure was developed more than three decades ago, the Internet was a much friendlier place, populated primarily by university researchers and scientists in search of easier collaboration. Little consideration was given to the medium's potential for corrupt marketing, fraud or transmission of anything as harmful as today's viruses. Fortunately new technologies that enable secure, trusted email are emerging as an "overlay" that operates in conjunction with SMTP to root out friend from foe.

Who Are You?

Knowing who is behind the email entering your network is essential to managing incoming email streams. ID falsification today stands at the heart of mounting concerns over email security. Indeed, the existing email architecture offers an open field for identity pirates to exploit its weaknesses for profit or to launch a devastating virus attack.

Email-borne security breaches are rooted in the current protocol's inability to provide verification of a message source's true identity. When a message is received at a mail gateway server, for example, the only thing about that message that can be known with certainty is the IP address of the server that sent or last relayed it. As a result, illicit email can be effectively laundered by routing it through legitimate IP addresses before final delivery. In effect, these electronic sleights of hand enable spam or virus traffickers to mask their identities and infiltrate the inboxes of unsuspecting recipients.

The Evolution of Filtering Technology

To combat the spammers' use of "hijacked" IP addresses, new protocols are emerging. The current proposals include standards called SPF (Sender Policy Framework), Caller ID, and

Domain Keys. They all revolve around the principle that an incoming email can be authenticated or positively tied back to the purported sender. Unfortunately, the technical complexities associated with email sender authentication are many, as evidenced by the fact that there are currently three separate proposals being circulated, each with its own strengths and weaknesses. Furthermore, widespread adoption of these protocols will take years.

FAST FACT:
The Domain Keys system is more advanced than Caller ID or Sender Policy Framework (SPF), but has the disadvantage of being more costly to implement.

However, the power of using a verifiable identity as a tool to combat spam and viruses is undeniable, thus the technical community continues to invest in enhanced sender authentication schemes. As these authentication systems mature, they will be a critical component of a comprehensive email security system.

Linking Sender Identity to Sender Reputation

As the mechanisms for authenticating the identity of email senders continue to evolve, the question remains, "So what?" Indeed, the mere authentication of a sender's identity is of questionable value if the sender and his reputation are unknown to the email recipient. So, while it's nice to know that a message is from XYZ Enterprises, do you really want the message if you are unfamiliar with XYZ and have no idea if it's a reputable mailer? The key, therefore, rests in the development of an email sender reputation service that can not only authenticate a sender's identity, but also characterize that identity's reputation as positive or negative based on sophisticated analysis of objective data. You still may not know exactly who XYZ is, but you can be assured of its track record as a reputable sender.

Reputation tracking services are among the most promising developments in the battle to secure our email against intrusive spam, viruses and fraud. An email reputation service tracks the sending patterns and behaviors of a given email sender. Effective reputation services pass no editorial judgment on a sender; they simply gather verifiable, measurable data on the sender's mailing patterns.

FAST FACT

SenderBase is a free service designed to help email administrators better manage incoming email streams by providing objective data about the identity of senders.

SenderBase from IronPort Systems is the industry's first and largest email sender traffic monitoring service.

Three Billion Updates Per Day
Paint a Powerful Picture

IronPort Systems launched SenderBase in 2003 as a critical tool in the fight against spam and other threats to email security, and is the only free and open email traffic monitoring service. The open-source software community has embraced SenderBase because it provides such rich data, which allows open-source, spam filtering programs such as Spam Assassin to make a more accurate assessment of a message's legitimacy. More than 28,000 networks today access SenderBase data as part of their spam filtering efforts. This translates into more than three billion machine queries per day. These queries are an important data source for SenderBase.

FAST FACT
Spammers send out hundreds of millions of email messages a day, while the largest corporations in the world send only a few million a day.

SenderBase Offers Numerous Information Parameters

SenderBase tracks more than 40 different information parameters on any given sender. These parameters include:

- The global volume of mail being sent

- How that volume has changed over time

- Low response rates

- Acceptance of returned mail

- The sender's country of origin

SenderBase has an "MX Spider" that, similar to a web page search engine, crawls the Internet to determine if a given IP address accepts mail or not. A mail source can also be probed to see if it is an infected machine, serving as an open proxy or open relay. Spammers frequently bounce their mail off these hijacked systems to obscure their identity. A high-volume mailer who has been mailing on an IP address for a only few hours or days is particularly suspect. Conversely, a mailer that has been sending reasonable volumes steadily for a long period of time is probably legitimate. In addition, SenderBase tracks more than 15 public blacklists and white-lists, as well as end-user complaint data.

How SenderBase Works

Any of these parameters could be considered circumstantial evidence. But when each parameter is considered in conjunction with another, interesting patterns emerge. SenderBase processes all of these data points, and more, in a statistical algorithm that produces sender scores that range from -10 (very untrustworthy) to +10 (very trustworthy). A sender's score is made available in real time to the IronPort Email Security Appliances, which use the rating to determine how to appropriately handle the message.

Variable Response to Spam

FAST FACT

Throttling is the adjustment of delivery rate depending on sender reputation scores.

The concept is simple: The more suspicious a sender's traffic patterns, the more restricted its access becomes to a receiver deploying an IronPort system.

First-generation systems had a black-or-white approach—messages were either "spam" or "not spam." Spammers skillfully manipulate these systems by appearing gray enough to slip past a computer's black-and-white analysis. A variable response, such as throttling based on reputation provides a much more robust defense to spam attacks. In other words, the recipient is empowered to account for the sender's shades of gray. An intelligent approach such as this accounts for shifting spammer tactics, yielding maximum effectiveness.

Preventive Response to Virus Outbreaks

The SenderBase email traffic data that powers IronPort's Reputation Filters can also be used to detect virus outbreaks before they penetrate traditional reactive defenses. Modern email viruses with cryptic names like *Netsky* and *Bagel* will propagate globally in less than two hours, bringing networks around the world to a halt. Traditional anti-virus systems need to capture the virus, analyze it in the lab, produce a digital signature or "definition" file, and then distribute these definition files, a process that takes six to eight hours.

IronPort's Virus Outbreak Filters act as a coarse outer layer of defense against viruses. Similar to a Reputation Filter that throttles or slows down suspicious spam senders, Virus Outbreak Filters "slow down" or quarantine suspicious message types. When the Global SenderBase network detects a sudden surge in suspicious messages—say password-protected .zip files—it raises the virus threat level indicator, causing the IronPort Email Security Appliances to quarantine suspicious messages until the reactive anti-virus filters have had time to update. The combination of a preventive system coupled with a reactive one yields maximum protection.

Legitimate Email Gets a Boost from Bonded Sender

While IronPort's SenderBase offers email receivers and mail administrators a way to distinguish legitimate sources of mail, another IronPort service, Bonded Sender, is helping legitimate emailers get their mail identified and delivered.

While some senders may generate suspicious sending patterns, their messages may be legitimate. Media companies or online retailers (e-tailers), for example, often dispense large volumes of similar-looking email in sudden bursts, while other legitimate senders may arouse suspicion simply because they've shifted IP addresses due to a change in their Internet collocation provider or some other infrastructure modification. As a result, their history of good email behavior may be lost. Or a legitimate sender may have low email volume rates, but still fall prey to unsophisticated spam filters based on the nature of their message content. Just imagine the problems encountered by legitimate Viagra suppliers!

FAST FACT
A "false-positive" is when a legitimate email is erroneously blocked by a filter.

First-generation spam filters—now widely deployed—have treated such senders poorly, resulting in what are commonly referred to as "false-positives," where legitimate mail is erroneously blocked. An assortment of high-profile false-positives has underscored the imprecision that continues to plague anti-spam warriors. Prominent examples include an email filter that trapped acceptance notifications to Harvard University applicants; a major ISP that blocked all mail to or from Russia on suspicion of spam; or another ISP that once blocked its own online billing notifications. In all fairness, most of us have had legitimate email stuck in the "junk" folder or, even worse, deleted.

The Email Equivalent of Pre-Paid Calling Cards

A solution rests in Bonded Sender, which operates like the pre-paid phone card of the email reputation world. Bonded Sender enables legitimate senders to "put their money where their mouths are" by posting a financial bond to guarantee their legitimacy. The concept is simple: Senders post a bond—say (US) $10,000—in an escrow account. Senders then can register an IP address that they control as legitimate, and signal ISPs not to spam filter mail from their bonded IP. If end-users complain that a message from the sender is spam, that sender's bond is debited at a rate of (US) $20 per complaint. The Bonded Sender Program has helped CNET successfully deliver more than 45 million emails per month to recipients. Through careful list management and awareness of consumer sensitivities, CNET successfully delivers tens of millions of messages to end users monthly, while consistently holding complaint rates to well below 0.5 complaints per million messages sent. This is nearly an order of magnitude lower than the Internet average of 4 complaints per million.

FAST FACT

More than 28,000 ISPs, corporations and universities, representing more than 25% of all Internet mailboxes, are participating in the Bonded Sender program.

Making Spammers Pay

Bonded Sender is more than just a useful tool for legitimate senders to identify themselves. It is a very practical way to fundamentally change the economics of spam. The reason there is such a deluge of spam is because the cost to send a message is measured in nano-cents. There have been many proposals to employ some type of postage stamp on email, and change the economics of the medium. The problem with these proposals is that there is no absolute way to identify spam from non-spam. That means the postage stamp would need to apply to all senders, making its adoption highly unlikely. Bonded Sender's novel approach harnesses the power of a market-based mechanism (spammers could never afford to pay (US) $20 per complaint—they'd be broke in a day), while not imposing an across-the-board tariff on all email users.

FAST FACT
Bonded Sender changes the economics of spam by requiring a sender to place a bond on their IP address and pay per complaint.

Applied economic tactics such as Bonded
Sender are expected to play an important role
in Microsoft's previously announced Coordinated
Spam Reduction Initiative, with Hotmail
and MSN among the largest ISPs to adopt the
program. That means IP addresses registered
with Bonded Sender will not be blocked by spam
filters at Hotmail, MSN or other major ISPs
such as Road Runner.

Let the Punishment Fit the Crime

Modern email security threats are adaptive,
mutating and ultimately powered by human cre-
ativity. Traditional static, rules-based approaches
will never win. Modern email security systems
must be intelligent enough to provide a variable
response that counters the perceived threat.
These modern systems must use emerging technologies such as Caller ID to establish the identity
of a sender. Furthermore, they must assess the
trustworthiness of the send based on the sender's
global traffic behavior. When an email perimeter
system is smart enough to know when to quarantine

a series of messages that might be a virus out-break or to throttle a new sender that might be sending spam, it can repeatedly adapt to today's evolving email threats.

QUICK LOOK

IP Address is the Basis of Identity in Email
Similar to your Social Security number, the IP address of your mail server is the basis of your email identity. New protocols like SPF and Caller ID will enhance identity verification, but will take years to be adopted.

Your Reputation Is Everything
The traffic patterns of a sender can readily expose friend from foe. Filters that examine the reputation of a given sender are very difficult for spammers to manipulate.

Traffic Patterns Even Reveal Virus Outbreaks
Examining global email traffic patterns can drive a highly effective preventive defense against virus outbreaks. This defense slows down or quarantines suspicious messages until the virus "cure" is ready.

Respond In Kind
Modern email security appliances must be intelligent enough to dynamically respond to changing email threats. Traffic monitoring systems can identify suspicious traffic patterns, but the receiving mail gateway must be able to rapidly accept or slow down senders' based on their apparent threat.

"Email is mission-critical to my business. Technology provides great tools to fight the email security battle. But there is no substitute for a solid understanding of the many management issues surrounding email."

MARK FITZGERALD
Messaging Manager, KeyCorp

9

CHECKPOINTS FOR THE FUTURE
KEEPING PACE WITH EMAIL'S EVOLUTION.

There are no silver bullets to eliminate email's flaws. The ultimate answer will likely emerge as a cocktail of many complementary solutions. Email's sustained viability demands a convergence not only in market-driven research and technological development, but also in email administrators' embrace of a new kind of transmission environment built on adopted best practices, sender identity verification and reputation authentication.

What You Should Do Next

The subsequent points and suggestions are critical to keep pace with email's continued evolution. If you follow these you'll take a significant step toward protecting your network, and your organization's hard-earned reputation.

▲ **Corporations should block all outgoing mail** that doesn't go through one of their SMTP email gateways. This allows IT staff to implement policy filtering on outgoing mail and dramatically reduce the spread of viruses. This outbound checkpoint is easily implemented using the corporate firewall to block all outbound port 25 traffic not coming from one of the designated mail gateways.

▲ **Carefully manage bounces.** Bounce messages should always be delivered as delayed bounces, which are separate emails sent to the sender that notify him or her of an invalid address. Bouncing messages during the SMTP conversation exposes the corporate directory to spammers looking to harvest valid addresses. Also, sophisticated commercial solutions have built-in defenses against directory harvest attacks, which stop accepting mail from a given sender if that sender has exceeded a certain number of invalid addresses. It's an important security safeguard.

▲ **Segment your traffic.** New generations of email gateways are able to place different classes of traffic on different outbound IP addresses. Use one set of IP addresses for transactional email, another for employee email, and yet another for bounce messages. If any of these various traffic

types induce deliverability problems, the IP seg-
mentation creates "watertight compartments"
that contain the damage only to that class of
traffic. The best example is the growing instance
of spammers sending messages with a bounce
address of a known spam trap. If the corporation
bounces the message, they end up on a blacklist
that can be very difficult to get off. If the traffic is
segmented, then the only thing that gets blocked
is the bounce IP, and corporate mail is unaffected.

☁ **Be aware of your reputation as a sender.** If your
company is doing any email marketing, check with
an email reputation service such as SenderBase
(www.senderbase.org) to measure the complaint
rates associated with the marketing mail.
Segmenting your traffic (see above) makes
it much easier to resolve marketing-generated
issues from employee-generated issues. Most
leading reputation services will have some type of
program that will provide a report that reflects how
major ISPs regard mail from your IP addresses.

☁ **Actively manage your reputation.** Publishing an
SPF or Caller ID record helps establish your legitimacy and prevents others from stealing your
identity. Listing your IP addresses with an email
accreditation service such as BondedSender
(www.bondedsender.org) can ensure that your mail

is delivered without risk of the occasional "false-positive," or deletion by a spam filter.

⬧ **Define a clear email retention and deletion policy.** Make certain that this policy is enforced consistently at the perimeter and on the message store. Many companies will define a 30-day retention policy only to find that the perimeter systems have been logging and archiving messages for two years.

⬧ **When defining email policies, make them specific** to certain groups within the company. For example, adding a disclaimer footer may be a global action, but scanning for a key word such as "proprietary" or "confidential" will yield very high false-positive rates unless it is put into a more fine-grained filter such as "scan all mail from engineering going to these five competitors for the following 20 words—proprietary, confidential, project x, project y, etc."

⬧ **Add defense-in-depth.** When deploying a traditional image-based virus filter, use different vendors at multiple layers. For example, use Symantec, NAI and Sophos at the desktop, message store and perimeter. Each vendor has its own techniques for detecting viruses, resulting in varying reaction times. Since no one vendor is always first, deploying separate vendors provides maximum protection.

- **Deploy a preventive security solution.** Preventive security systems detect suspicious traffic patterns and then quarantine suspicious attachment types that are associated with an outbreak. These systems are very effective at stopping rapid outbreak viruses such as *SoBig, Netsky* and *Klez.* An improvement in reaction time of several hours can translate into millions of dollars saved on cleanup of desktop systems.

- **Spam filter technology gets stale relatively quickly.** Systems that use keywords or filtering techniques such as Bayesian analysis can be defeated easily by spammers who use modified keywords (V1AGRA) or by attaching "bayz busting" blocks of text. These blocks of text contain seemingly random words that Bayesian filters correlate with legitimate email, enabling spam to get through. The best commercial spam solutions use real-time updates to stay ahead of spam without inducing false-positives.

- **When evaluating commercial email security** vendors, choose one that is leading the development of new email standards. The email infrastructure is evolving rapidly to adapt to the growing threats.

Don't make an investment in a solution that won't be able to speak the language of tomorrow's identity-enabled email infrastructure.

The Future Is Now

A new generation of applications will convert sending and receiving gateways into efficient checkpoints, where mail will either earn the imprimatur of legitimacy, or be cast aside as non-compliant. In other words, emailers who don't play by the rules simply won't play.

AFTERWORD
DID YOU GET THE MESSAGE?

The Times They Are a Changin'

The preceding chapters have defined the email environment: how it works, the issues facing it and some solutions to its evident shortcomings. As demonstrated every day with each message sent or received, email's value as a communications tool is undeniable. And it is that value that will ensure delivery of lasting solutions to existing weaknesses in the current email system.

It's easy to take for granted the sweeping changes in the workplace that are fueled by email. Yet it wasn't long ago when writing an inter-office memo was considered onerous, while distributing it, tracking it and accessing it days or months later was even more difficult. Email, thankfully, has made information exchange fluid and nearly frictionless. For many companies, email is the foundation of the paperless office, with records, notes, interviews, data and correspondence easily stored in their email systems. A change of this magnitude takes time to permeate into the deepest parts of our economy, but there is no question email usage will continue to flourish as the next generation of managers—who grew up using email —comes of age.

Despite email's widespread adoption, problems persist. While the impact of new federal legislation to check the tide of spam remains suspect on a practical level, its passage reflects a critical awareness of the need to safeguard email's future. Email's increasing role in regulatory compliance and legal discovery, not to mention the persistence of email-borne virus attacks and other security threats, are also adding to the market's appreciation of the medium's complexity and the need for focused email management.

Email Can Be Saved

The threats to email are as real as the promise email holds to improve the way business is conducted. As a result, the email infrastructure will go through a period of revolutionary change in coming years. Identity mechanisms such as Microsoft's Caller ID or SPF will be widely deployed. Receivers will put increasingly tight restrictions on mail from senders with unknown or poor reputations. The new email infrastructure won't activate immediately, but organizations that send email need to be aware of the changes that are occurring. If they ignore these changes, they will find themselves on the outside as protocols and practices evolve. This will mean the capability and reliability of their email use will become less and less effective. And that day is coming soon.

The cost of this change is enormous. A massive quantity of the world's email infrastructure will need to be replaced in the next five years. But the next-generation systems that get deployed will safeguard the medium as it continues to dramatically affect all of our lives.

GLOSSARY

The following glossary defines some commonly used terms and acronyms associated with the email environment.

A

Arpanet The precursor to the modern Internet, ARPAnet was an experimental network of computers created by the Advanced Research Projects Agency of the U.S. Department of Defense in the late 1960s to facilitate information exchange between research scientists.

B

Blacklist Any database that identifies the IP addresses known to be used by spammers. ISPs and email administrators used blacklists as first-generation anti-spam systems. Many are still in operation today.

Bonded Sender Sponsored by IronPort Systems, the Bonded Sender program enables legitimate email originators to post a financial bond to ensure the integrity of their email campaigns. Recipients who feel they have received an unsolicited email from a Bonded Sender can complain to their ISP, enterprise, or IronPort and a financial charge is debited from the bond. The Bonded Sender program helps email-senders ensure that their messages get to their end-users, and provides corporate IT managers and ISPs with an objective way to ensure that only unwanted messages get blocked.

C

CAN Spam Act The federal Controlling the Assault of Non-Solicited Pornography and Marketing Act of 2003 (CAN Spam) establishes administrative, civil and criminal guidelines to help consumers and businesses protect themselves from unsolicited commercial email, otherwise known as spam.

D

Domain A group of networked computers administered under the same guidelines. Domains are identified by their IP addresses.

DNS Domain Name Servers translate domain names into IP addresses to enable message transmission.

F

Filename Extension (COM, EXE, etc.) Typically preceded by a period, or dot, extensions are added to the end of a message file name to indicate the type of information contained in that file.

Firewall A hardware or software system that screens or blocks messages coming into or leaving a private computer network.

FTP File Transfer Protocol is a simple means for transferring files via the Internet. The protocol enables users to log on to a remote site, obtain files and transfer them to their computer.

G

Gateway The network computer that provides access to and from another network. In email, the gateway is a server that speaks SMTP and does the job of accepting and queuing incoming messages and routing them to the appropriate message store. For outgoing email, the email gateway also manages connections to receiving gateway servers at remote ISPs.

H

Harvesting   The act of covertly collecting email addresses for compilation of email databases to be used for unsolicited mailings.

HTML   Hypertext Markup Language is used to create documents transmitted over the World Wide Web. It deploys a range of tags to define a document's structure and layout.

HTTP   Hypertext Transfer Protocol is the prevailing file-exchange system that underlies the World Wide Web. It determines how a message is formatted and sent, and the actions of browsers and servers in response to given commands.

I

IMAP   Internet Message Access Protocol, like POP, is a common protocol used to retrieve email from an email message store server. IMAP allows an email client to store messages locally and be used "offline" without connection to the message store.

Internet   A decentralized, global network linking computers for the exchange of data, messages, news and information.

IP Address Internet Protocol addresses are unique numbers assigned to each computer that is connected to the Internet. Messages are routed based on their destination's IP address.

ISP Internet Service Providers supply access to the Internet.

M

Message Store The Message Store is the general name for the mail server that stores end-user email. These servers use either the POP or IMAP protocols, or proprietary protocols found in commercial message stores such as Microsoft Exchange or Lotus Notes.

MTA (Message Transfer Agent) The MTA or email gateway (see Gateway definition) is the software that handles the actual delivery of an email.

P

POP Post Office Protocol, like IMAP, is a common protocol used to retrieve email from an email server. POP requires a live connection to the message store to manipulate mail messages.

S

SenderBase Powered by IronPort Systems, SenderBase is an email traffic monitoring database designed to help email administrators research senders, identify legitimate sources of email and block spammers.

SMTP Simple Mail Transfer Protocol is the principal protocol for relaying email between servers. SMTP functions in much the same way as a standard mail envelope, which features destination and return addresses. Using SMTP language embedded in each message's header, SMTP servers deliver and receive mail without having to examine the body of that message to determine its source or destination.

Spam Broadly defined as unsolicited commercial email, spam is estimated to account for roughly 70 percent of all email traffic.

Spam Trap Using an email address that's never been used by an individual, blacklist operators deploy spam traps on web pages and Internet discussion boards to catch spammers, who routinely create automatic programs or "crawlers" to course through web pages and harvest email addresses.

Spyware   Typically packaged as part of some ostensibly legitimate software that once downloaded and run, spyware spies on its host's Internet habits for use in directing advertising solicitations. It may also be referred to as Adware.

T

Trojan Horse   Programs disguised as something desirable, but that actually perform something terrible such as erasing a hard drive.

V

Virus   A chunk of parasitic software code that propagates each time an infected program is run, damaging or destroying other files and programs on the same computer.

W

World Wide Web   A network of Internet servers that process HTML documents and support access to other text, graphics or multimedia files.

Worm   Opportunistic programs engineered to move about in search of security holes in software or operating systems. Once inside, the worm replicates itself quickly to infiltrate other machines throughout a computer network.

ABOUT THE AUTHOR

TOM GILLIS is a recognized leader in the dynamically charged and high growth email security industry, with in-depth knowledge of the challenges surrounding secure network infrastructure. An influential and frequent conference and panel presenter, Gillis has made invaluable contributions to the email community including the SMTPi framework for secure email. Gillis has held positions at iBEAM Broadcasting, SGI, and Boston Consulting Group (BCG). He is currently the Chief Marketing Officer for IronPort Systems. *Get the Message* is his first book.